Book Cover Design from East Asia

T0343117

FIRST PUBLISHED 2016 ISBN 978-0-9570816-9-7

DESIGN Leterme Dowling

Forward

'Book Cover Design from East Asia' is a compilation of more than 100 book covers from this region.

Comprising China, Japan, Korea, Taiwan and Vietnam, societies in East Asia have historically been part of the Chinese cultural sphere and East Asian vocabulary and scripts are often derived from classical Chinese and Chinese scripts.

Chinese characters constitute one of the oldest continuously used systems of writing in the world and they are deeply rooted in this country's history. In standard Chinese they are called 'hanzi' but they have also been adapted to write a number of other languages including: Japanese, where they are known as 'kanji', Korean, where they are known as 'hanja', and Vietnamese in a system known as 'chữ Nôm'.

The art of calligraphy in China was the means by which scholars could mark their thoughts and teachings on philosophy and although function dominated the evolution of Chinese characters, it can not displace the beauty inherent in their aesthetic.

The relationship between typography and book design in China is inextricably linked. In the 12th Century, the decoration of traditional Chinese books, which were bound with string, consisted primarily of a title inscription by a calligrapher and imagery, if any, was usually unrelated to the story. The great boom in Chinese publishing, during the early decades of the 20th century, was due in part to a general increase in literacy, but also to a growing middle class in search of leisure pursuits. During this period, Western style books with glued or stapled bindings became common in China. The change to Western book formats from string bound books was an important step in the development of book design. Covers began to be thought of as an integral part of the book and graphic artists, inspired by European and American trends, were employed by publishing houses, as apposed to classically-trained painters and illustrators. Such designers were committed to recreating these age-old logograms and combining them with bold graphics.

There's something very alluring, in particular, about the design of East Asian book covers that I can't quite put my finger on and I have often found myself asking why design from this region in general speaks so clearly to so many people all over the world? I think this can be attributed, in part, to the use of restraint and economy, whether it's a kimono, a carefully raked garden path or a contemporary work of art.

When it comes to book cover art we see an equally careful aesthetic, often culminating on the shelf in a unified cultural voice. The covers, often austere in appearance, are confident in their use of restraint, with whitespace adorned with well considered marks of ink. Their colour is pared back, with one or two colours often the preference and their photography is artistic and subtle.

In fact, the vast majority of covers held within this book fall under this careful aesthetic.

Having studied the best in contemporary book cover design from East Asia over the last year, this has helped shed new light on the book covers we see in the West. In contrast, our designs seem far more hectic, chaotic even. And as you trace back through the history of book cover design in the West, there's a sense that it's getting visually louder.

With bookstores diminishing in the West at a rapid rate it is perhaps unsurprising as there will clearly be more competition for our attention on the shelf. This results in an ever escalating shouting match between covers.

However, the silver lining is that with the present digital revolution in our buying experience, the role of the cover is changing radically. It simply doesn't need to shout anymore because the cover doesn't serve the same purpose. Strangely, book readers can thank Amazon for this newfound liberation. Book covers now appear next to titles and the author's name and designers are less expected to promote the same kind of information hierarchy — image making is now trumping legibility and the need for simple, striking graphics is more imperative than ever when the book cover is condensed down to a thumbnail.

Let's be honest though, we all judge a book by its cover most of the time. Each of us is exposed to several thousand messages a day and to be successful, whether online or in store, covers not only have to stand out amongst all the clutter, but they also need to make an instant connection with viewers. In short, book covers have to do a lot of work and designing them isn't an easy task.

With millions of books being published each year, you need something special to jump out from the crowd and force the reader to pick up the book. The great covers draw you in through their cleverness, simplicity or boldness and an effective book cover manages to catch the eye and to convey the idea behind the book on one single page. It's the first thing you see and a great cover can persuade you to start that journey of discovery, page by page.

What these covers have in common, regardless of their region, is a shared serenity and balance that resonates beautifully with their simple, uncluttered and modern aesthetic.

The main idea of this book is to provide you with examples of some creative, expressive and appealing book covers from some of the most important East Asian designers working today.

There's no exact formula. Some whisper, others scream. Much like crafting the perfect calligraphy, learning to design a great book cover takes dedication, love and the desire to be bold.

Jon Dowling
COUNTER-PRINT

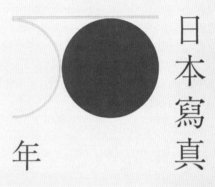

Source: 8

日本寫真

50

年

照片的力量。
言語的力量。
生存的力量。

森山大道
中平卓馬
荒木經惟
篠山紀信
佐內正史
藤代冥紗
長島有里枝
蜷川實花
大橋仁
Takashi Homma

攝影就是「生命・機器・外在」間的搏鬥現場。
透過十位當代攝影家的生命經驗、工作思考
進入兼具意識與無意識的渾沌眾生相——「日本寫真」

大竹昭子……著　黃大旺……譯　王志弘 平面設計師……選書・設計　張世倫 阿諾草／黃亞紀 布安藍蘭台北負責人……視覺

TITLE 50 Years of Japanese Photography
PUBLISHER Faces Publishing

京極夏彥

冥

談

KYOGOKU NATSUHIKO

「怪」KWAI
BOOKS

冥談
めいだん

京極夏彥繼《幽談》後，
再度帶來散發妖異光芒的
全新現代怪談。

王華懋◎譯

那是是難忘別死者誓言的屋子，
在前往那兒的路上，不論你想起了什麼，千萬別說出來……

不可思議的空間，曖昧模糊的記憶
在生與死的兩端精心打造的記憶迷宮
——你，找得到出口嗎？

作者巧妙了恐怖故事如何在現代延續的重大命題，在日常的風景中，他創造出日本怪談的新境界。——陳國偉 中興大學台灣文學經對教授

生死
疲劳
劳

life and
death are
wearing
me out

*A wildly visceral and
creative novel ...
A vast, crazi,
and complex story.
–The New York Times
Book Review*

莫言

mo
yan

*Nobel Prize
for Literature
2012*

a novel

長島有里枝

nagashima yurie

背景的の記憶

source no. 10   faces publications

Wang, Zhi-Hong

9

TITLE Memories of You PUBLISHER Faces Publishing

二十一世紀

ACROPOLIS
衛城

LE CAPITAL AU XXIᵉ SIÈCLE
THOMAS PIKETTY

托瑪・皮凱提——著 詹文碩・陳以禮——譯

資本論

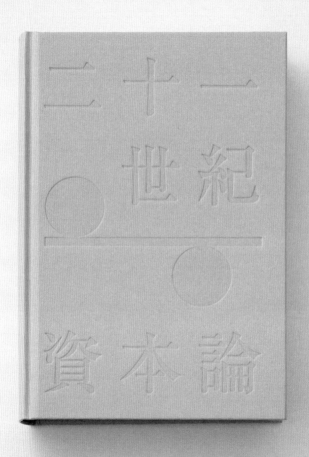

PUBLIC

Michael Sandel can always be
counted on to write with
elegance and intelligence about
important things. Whether you
agree or not, you cannot ignore
his arguments. We need all the
sane voices we can get in the
public square and Sandel's is one
of the sanes.

**JEAN BETHKE ELSHTAIN,
THE UNIVERSITY OF CHICAGO
DIVINITY SCHOOL**

PHILOSOPHY

ESSAYS
ON MORALITY
IN POLITICS

MICHAEL
J. SANDEL

RYE FIELD
PUBLICATIONS

為什麼
我們需要
公共哲學
：
政治中的
道德問題

邁可‧桑德爾 —— 著　　蔡惠伃‧林詠心 —— 譯

TITLE Theory of Corruption PUBLISHER Rye Field Publishing

TITLE Frog PUBLISHER Rye Field Publishing

KASHIWA SATO

SAMURAI（サムライ）/ 佐藤可士和
Creative Studio
Art Director·Creative Director

你 是
林徽因作品全集

人 间 的

四 月 天

You are the April of this World
The Complete Works of Lin Huiyin

Lin Huiyin 林徽因

VOL. 1 文学卷　　VOL. 2 建筑卷
Literature　　　Architecture

天津出版传媒集团
天津人民出版社

Akira 黑澤 明

日 本 を 代 表 す る 映 画 監 督

Kurosawa

蝦蟆的油

蝦蟇の油

ガマ

蝦蟆の油

蕭傑美士 訳

侯孝賢 監演 — 推薦人 — 影評 聞天祥

CNN評選 20世紀亞洲最有貢獻人物 藝文類

日本民間故事有這樣一個故事：在深山裡，有一種特別的蝦蟆，不僅外表奇醜無比，而且還多了三幾條腿，人們抓到牠後，將其放在鏡子前或玻璃箱內，蝦蟆一看到自己醜陋不堪的外表不禁嚇出一身油。這種油，也是民間用來治療燒傷燙傷的珍貴藥材。

晚年回首往事，黑澤明自喻猶如站在鏡子前的蝦蟆，發現自己拍過的種種不堪之處，一身油。自傳故事名為《蝦蟆的油》，是一代電影巨匠的直面人生的真摯告白。……《蝦蟆的油：黑澤明尋找黑澤明》(Something Like an Autobiography by Akira Kurosawa)

枕草子

The Pillow Book
by
Sei Shōnagon

TITLE The Pillow Book PUBLISHER Horizon

the
食 herbivorous 草
家 family 族

winner of the nobel prize
in literature

a novel

rye field
publication.

莫 mo yan 言

TITLE The Herbivorous Family
PUBLISHER Rye Field Publishing

TITLE Shashin No Hanashi
PUBLISHER Ecus Publishing

TITLE Sandalwood Death
PUBLISHER Rye Field Publishing

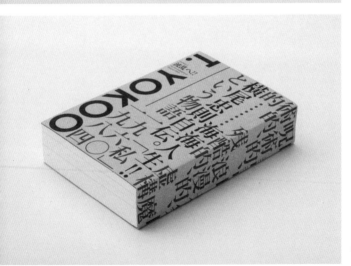

TITLE The Autobiography of Tadanori Yokoo
PUBLISHER Faces Publishing

↑

How to Design

いちばん面白い
デザインの
教科書

カイシトモヤ 著

ぼくが現場から
デザインのやり方、教えます。

造形の基本／配色のセオリー／文字と書体
写真と画像処理／レイアウトの考え方／印刷の知識

「どう考えて、どう手を動かすのか。」
グラフィックデザインの現場で求められる基礎知識とデジタルスキルを
実践的なプロセスとともにわかりやすく解説。

MdN
エムディエヌコーポレーション
www.MdN.co.jp

Arata Kubota

22

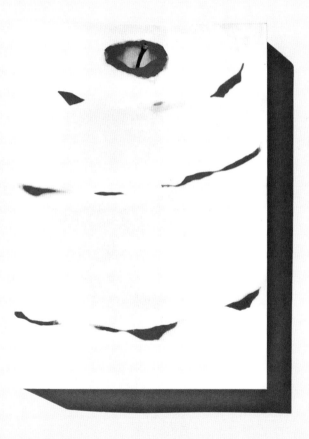

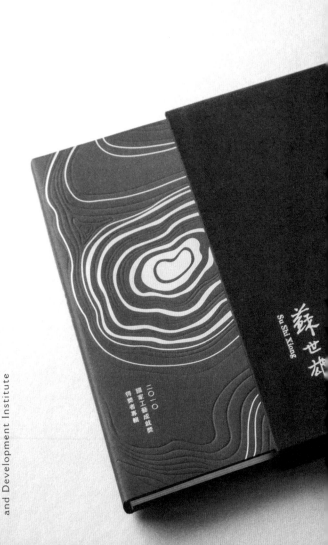

TITLE Su Shi Xiong Monograph
PUBLISHER National Taiwan Craft Research
and Development Institute

蘇世雄
Su Shi Xiong

二〇一〇
國家工藝成就獎
得獎者專輯

雕釉之美

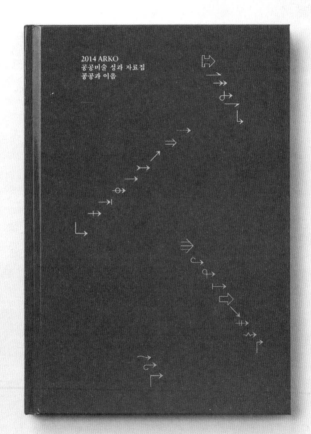

The Power of Images

The
National
Museum
of
Ethnology
Collection

イメージの力
——国立民族学博物館コレクションにさぐる

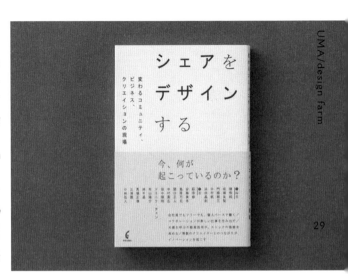

TITLE Designing Share: Emerging Community, Business, Creation PUBLISHER Gakugei Shuppansha

TITLE Yohkoso Yohkoso: Redrawing the Design PUBLISHER Gakugei Shuppansha

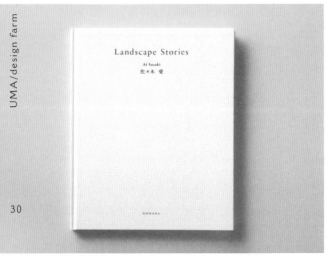

TITLE Ai Sasaki: Landscape Stories
PUBLISHER Nohara

↑

ミメーシスの詩学

安東伸介著述集

ARS POETICA: Discourses and Writings of Shinsuke ANDO

「慶應英文学」の継承

西脇順三郎、
厨川文夫の薫陶を受け、
慶應義塾で長く教鞭を執った、
希代の英文学者による著述集。
チョーサー、シェイクスピア、
そして福澤諭吉や
義塾ゆかりの人々をめぐって、
その洒脱な「語り」がいま、
鮮やかによみがえる。

慶應義塾大学出版会　定価〔本体3,200円＋税〕

ベルリン 花代

ベルリン

花代

花代の過ごしたベルリン。
15年にもわたる、いつもおなじドイツでの日々。
花代が出会ったハンナとの愉快で、
かけがえのない仲間たちとの軌跡。

月曜社

月曜社

TITLE Berin Hanayos Saugeile Kumpels
PUBLISHER Getsuyosha Limited

TITLE Have a Go at Flying from Music
PUBLISHER Printed as Manuscript

TITLE Shigeo Toya Sculptures and Texts
PUBLISHER NOHARA

suyama design

34

TITLE Kichi ha Naze Okinawa ni
Syuchushiterunoka PUBLISHER NHK Publishing

TITLE Nikka: A Book of Kyoto Japanese
Sweets PUBLISHER Seigensha

ポール・エリュアール
絵 オードリー・フォンドゥカヴ
訳 須山 実

text
paul eluard
art work
audrey fondecave
translation
minoru suyama

grain-d'aile
グランデール

TITLE Yanomami PUBLISHER NHK Publishing

TITLE Study in Green PUBLISHER Gettosha

TITLE Portolano PUBLISHER SAYUSHA

Nakano Design Office Co., Ltd

38

title Architect of 12 Groups of 13
publisher LIXIL Corporation

伊東豊雄
伊丹潤
柳澤孝彦
長谷川逸子
谷口吉生
山本理顕
象設計集団　樋口裕康　富田玲子
坂本一成
鈴木恂
石山修武
東孝光
安藤忠雄

十二組十三人の建築家

古谷誠章対談集

古谷誠章、
モダニズム
最後の地平を超えて

明治神宮
以前以後

以前・
以後

近代神社を
めぐる
環境形成の
構造転換

藤田大誠
青井哲人
畔上直樹
今泉宜子 編

明治神宮
以前以後

近代神社を
めぐる
環境形成の
構造転換

藤田大誠
青井哲人
畔上直樹
今泉宜子 編

近代日本において国家的・
公共的な存在とされた神社。

変貌してゆく都市や地域社
会のなかで、それはどのよ

うな機能や特質をもつ空間
として創出され、いかなる

環境・風致・景観が創出さ
れようとしたのか。一大

近代的の明治神宮造営と大
きなメルクマールと捉え

神道史、建築史、都市史
地域社会史ほか、神社境内の

環境形成をめぐるダイナ
ミックな構造転換を描く。

TITLE Before and After Meiji-Jingu

PUBLISHER Kajima Institute Publishing

Nakano Design Office Co., Ltd

40

TITLE Gakken Kagaku-sensho

PUBLISHER Gakken Education Publishing Co., Ltd.

Nakano Design Office Co., Ltd

42

TITLE Kiyoo Kawamura Exhibition
PUBLISHER Meguro Museum of Art, Tokyo

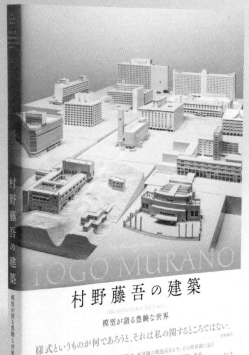

Nakano Design Office Co., Ltd

43

TITLE The Prolific World of Togo Murano

Architectural Models PUBLISHER Seigensha Art

Publishing, Inc.

村野藤吾の建築

ARCHITECTURAL MODELS

模型が語る豊饒な世界

様式というものが何であろうと、それは私の関するところではない。

村野藤吾

建築の「原罪」を考え続けた村野藤吾。再評価の機運高まる今、その世界観に迫る

精巧模型、設計原図、村野の言葉、対談（長谷川堯 松隈洋）、掲載

青幻舎

TOGO MURANO

TITLE Basic Infographics PUBLISHER BNN, Inc.

TITLE Rise of the DEO (Japanese Edition)
PUBLISHER BNN, Inc.

TITLE This is Service Design Thinking PUBLISHER BNN, Inc.

TITLE Open Design PUBLISHER O'Reilly Japan

TITLE Layout and Colours: For Sales Promotion
PUBLISHER BNN, Inc.

セールを アピールする
レイアウト & カラーズ

注目を集めるためのキャンペーン・セールのデザイン事例集

● **PART 1.** ビジュアル展開 ● **PART 2.** ポスター ● **PART 3.** ショッパー・DM・チラシ

LAYOUT &
COLOURS

04

for SALES PROMOTION

BNN

写真で アピールする レイアウト＆カラーズ

写真を効果的に使った雑誌・カタログのデザイン事例集

● PART 1. 裁ち落とし　● PART 2. 角版　● PART 3. 切り抜き

LAYOUT &
COLOURS
03

by PHOTOGRAPH

BNN

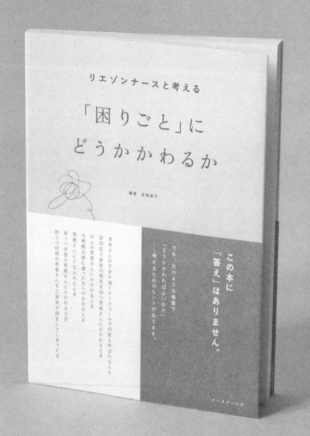

リエゾンナースと考える

「困りごと」に
どうかかわるか

編著 広瀬百子

この本に
「答え」はありません。

でも、次のような場面で
「どうかかわればよいのか」
考えるためのヒントがあります。

患者さんの不安が強くナースコールで何度も呼ばれるとき
認知症で身体の病気を持つ患者さんにかかわるとき
がんの患者さんにかかわるとき
大規模災害に遭った方にかかわるとき
患者さんになられたとき
抑うつ状態の患者さんにかかわるとき
抑うつ状態の患者さんをご家族が励ましてしまうとき

ナースツールズ

飛騨の森で

つくる？

TITLE Tsukuru? PUBLISHER Planning Section, Sightseeing Division, Hida City

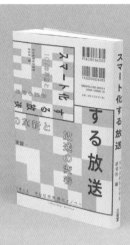

TITLE Anti-Intellectualism in Japanese Society
PUBLISHER Shobunsha

犀の教室
Liberal Arts Lab
晶文社

内田樹編

日本の反知性主義

赤坂真理
小田嶋隆
白井聡
想田和弘
高橋源一郎
仲野徹
名越康文
平川克美
鷲田清一

Anti-Intellectualism
in Japanese Society

街場の憂国会議

日本はこれから
どうなるのか

犀の教室
Liberal Arts Lab
晶文社

内田樹 編

小田嶋隆
想田和弘
高橋源一郎
中島岳志
中野晃一
平川克美
孫崎享
鷲田清一

TITLE Convention of Patriotism for People

PUBLISHER Shobunsha

CITY BOOK OF
BERLIN
ベルリン

BERLIN

現地クリエイターが教えてくれた
ベルリンの遊び方

ミッテ クロイツベルク ノイケルン フレンツラウアーベルク シャルロッテンブルク
ベルリン主要5エリアの詳細な地図と約300のスポットを紹介

改訂新版

100万円の
家づくり
自分でつくる木の棲み家

小笠原昌憲

晶文社

TITLE How to Build a House for Only One Million Yen (Revised Edition) PUBLISHER Shobunsha

日本のカタチ 2050

「こうなったらいい未来」の描き方

2050年の日本
エコハウスとエネルギー
竹内昌義

人口9500万人
都市と地方のリノベーション
馬場正尊

働き方・生き方は
あたらしい政治とメディア
マエキタミヤコ

どうなっている？
コミュニティデザイン
山崎亮

晶文社
社会
ライフスタイル

こんなまちに住みたいナ

絵本が育む暮らし・まちづくりの発想

延藤安弘

晶文社

内田 樹

こんな日本でよかったね

構造主義的日本論

「構造主義」がわかると
ちがう日本が見えてくる

「少子化問題」は存在しません！　日本は「辺境」で「属国」、それで何か問題でも？　これから目指すべきは「フェミニンな共産主義」です！　……あまりの暴論ぶりに思わず納得、"寝ながら学んだ"構造主義者・ウチダ先生による、驚愕の日本社会論。

自分イノベーション

Innovate Yourself

問題発見・解決の究極メソッド

林志行

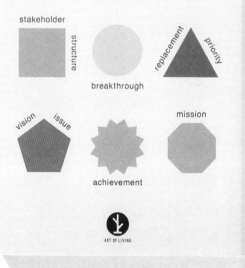

TITLE Innovate Yourself
PUBLISHER Gijutsu-Hyohron Sha

TITLE My House PUBLISHER Akishobo

TITLE Learning Supportive Psychotherapy:
An Illustrated Guide PUBLISHER Igaku Shoin

アジアの辺境に学ぶ幸福の質

瀬川正仁

People who live in
the remote areas of Asia
know what is
the hapiness.

辺境の民は、
わたしたち日本人？

いくらお金を稼いでも、埋められな
い不安と息苦しさ。そろそろヤメに
しませんか。大幅な経済成長が望
めない日本にとって、手本となるの
は欧米諸国ではなく、むしろ熱帯
アジアの国々。時間や規則に縛ら
れすぎない。老後の心配もしない
……。ゆるーい未来を探しましょう。

亜紀書房

人はお金がなくても生きていける。

TITLE People Who Live in the Remote Areas of Asia Know What Happiness is PUBLISHER Akishobo

ニッポンの個人情報

「個人を特定する情報が個人情報である」
と信じているすべての方へ

鈴木正朝
高木浩光
山本一郎

プライバシーフリーク、参上。

築土構木
の思想

土木で日本を建てなおす　藤井聡

青木泰樹
大石久和
柴山桂太
中野剛志
三橋貴明

土木を語らずして、国の未来を語るなかれ！

政治・経済、ナショナリズム、安全保障等の
観点から徹底検証。土木による日本再建論！

1土木学会
2014年、100周年 記念

蛍の教室
[政治・社会]

「踊り場」日本論

小田嶋隆　岡田憲治

停滞か成長か、勝ち負けじゃなくて、
中庸ってのも、あるでしょ。

ヘイトスピーチ、無意味なレッテル貼り……大きな声は目立つ
けど、穏やかでフツーの隣人もたくさんいる。日本でもっとも
穏健なコラムニストと、もっとも良心的な政治学者が吼える。

犀の教室
Liberal Arts Lab
［政治・社会］

TITLE Revive Japan!: Public Philosophy in Our Neighborhood PUBLISHER Gijutsu-Hyohron Sha

TITLE Rise of Corporate Generated Media PUBLISHER Gijutsu-Hyohron Sha

失敗は「そこ」から はじまる

Sidetracked

フランチェスカ・ジーノ［著］ 柴田裕之［訳］

コカ・コーラ、サムスン、ヤフー創業者……綿密に計画したはずなのに、

「あの人、あの会社が、 なんでそんなことを?」

ハーバード・ビジネススクール人気教授が提言する意思決定「9つの原則」

ダイヤモンド社

藤井聡

21世紀の全体主義

〈凡庸〉という悪魔

ハンナ・アーレントの
全体主義論で読み解く
現代日本の病理構造

言論を封殺する政治家、思考停止の官僚・学者たちに屈しないために！

TITLE DEZACON 2013 in Yonago Official Book
PUBLISHER Kenchiku Shiryo Kenkyusya CO.,LTD.

TITLE Ryuseiha Hanatecho PUBLISHER Ryuseiha

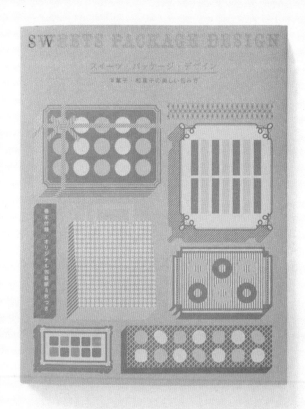

TITLE Sweets Package Design
PUBLISHER Graphic-sha Publishing Co., Ltd.

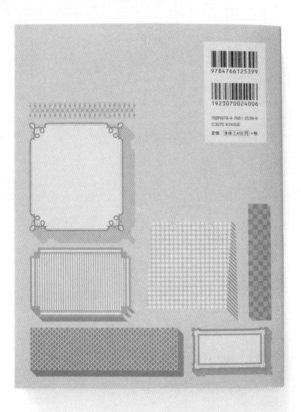

9784766125399

1923070024006

ISBN978-4-7661-2539-9
C3070 ¥2400E

定価 本体2,400円＋税

←

Motoi Shito

72

TITLE A Journey Through Monochrome Illustrations
PUBLISHER BNN, Inc.

モノクロ絵の世界

**A Journey Through
Monochrome
Illustrations**

**A Journey Through
Monochrome
Illustrations**

ISBN978-4-86100-989-1

C3070 ¥2600E

定価：本体2,800円＋税

ピー・エヌ・エヌ新社

9784861009891

1923070026000

←

74

PUBLISHER Seoul Foundation for Arts and Culture

TITLE Diverland

TITLE With You, I'll Never Feel Lonely
PUBLISHER Time Zone 8

↑

TITLE How Future Parallels Reality!
PUBLISHER Wenzhi Books

TITLE Yan Cong Collage 2014
PUBLISHER Star Gallery

TITLE The Book to Start a Small Business
Suitable for Yourself

Tatsu Shoseki Co.,Ltd.

↑

TITLE Genzaichi vol.1

PUBLISHER NHK Publishing, Inc.

↑

TITLE Invisible Hand of Data
PUBLISHER Soshisha Publishing Co.,Ltd.

↑

TITLE The Complete Works of Mineo Kato 'Showa no Tokyo' PUBLISHER Deco

↑

本にせざるを得ないっ!

アボカド塩辛・生ラー油の生みの親
うおつかさんの6年間の料理日記から厳選!
作って食べられるおいしいエッセイ

キノブックス

TITLE Night Lights PUBLISHER Seigensya

TITLE Birth 100 Years: Yazaki Hironobu
Exhibition : Beyond the Footage

BRUNO MUNARI
ブルーノ・ムナーリのファンタジア

ブルーノ・ムナーリのファンタジア
BRUNO MUNARI

創造力ってなんだろう

TITLE Bruno Munari
PUBLISHER Vangi Sculpture Garden Museum

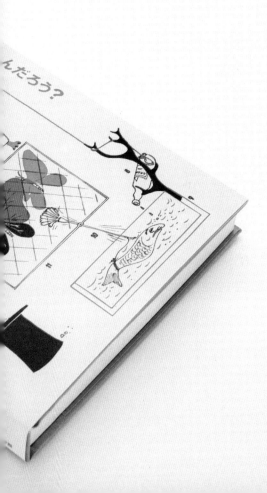

世界の模様帖

テキスタイルにみる伝承デザイン

江馬 進 著

青幻舎
SEIGENSHA

A Book of World Textile Designs
Traditional Textile Designs

世界の模様帖

テキスタイルにみる伝承デザイン

江馬 進 著

SEKAI

NO

MOYO

CHO

青幻舎
SEIGENSHA

TITLE A Book of World Textile Designs
PUBLISHER Seigensha Art Publishing

TITLE The End of the Journey the Beginning of the Location PUBLISHER IROHA PUBLISHING

IROHA PUBLISHING

僕らはまだ、世界を1ミリも知らない

――けど、その知らない世界がオモシロイ！Travel the world as a liberal arts !!!

リアルを知る最高の教科書である

この本は世界のリアルを知る最高の教科書である

――四角大輔

著：School With 代表

太田英基

2年50ヵ国、1000人以上のビジネスマンたちと出逢ってきた起業家の世界一周の記録から学ぶ、グローバル世代の知識と教養

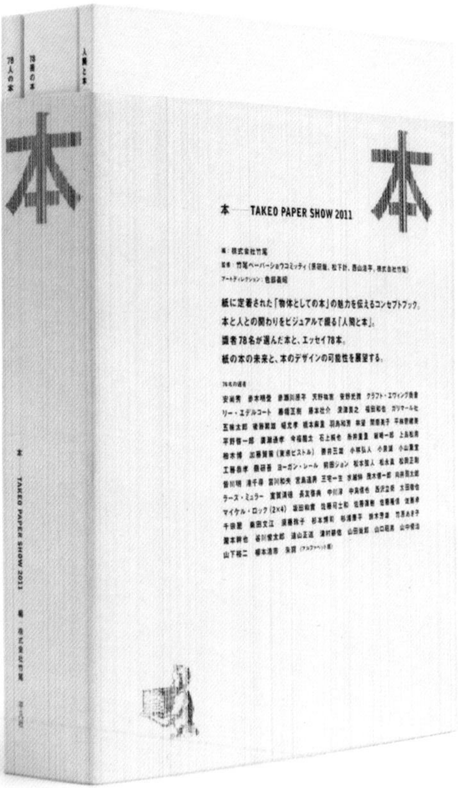
78人の本
78冊の本
人間と本
本
本
本 TAKEO PAPER SHOW 2011
紙に定着された「物体としての本」の魅力を伝えるコンセプトブック。
本と人との関わりをビジュアルで綴る「人間と本」。
読者78名が選んだ本と、エッセイ78本。
紙の本の未来と、本のデザインの可能性を展望する。
TAKEO PAPER SHOW 2011

TITLE ‘Book’ Takeo Paper Show 2011
PUBLISHER Heibonsha Limited, Publishers

Yoshiaki Irobe /
Nippon Design Center, Inc.

年鑑日本の空間デザイン
2011

ディスプレイ・サイン・商環境

Annual of Space
Design in Japan 2011

Displays, Signs &
Commercial Spaces

六耀社

TITLE Annual of Space Design in Japan 2011

PUBLISHER Rikuyosha Co., Ltd

TITLE Annual of Space Design in Japan 2014
PUBLISHER Rikuyosha Co., Ltd

年鑑
日本の空間
デザイン
2014

ディスプレイ・サイン・商環境

Annual of Space Design in Japan 2014

Displays, Signs & Commercial Spaces

Rikuyosha

六耀社

Yoshiaki Irobe /
Nippon Design Center, Inc.

年鑑
日本の空間
デザイン
2015 六耀社

Annual of Spacial Design in Japan 2015
Rikuyosha

TITLE Annual of Spacial Design in Japan 2015
PUBLISHER Rikuyosha Co., Ltd

Yoshiaki Irobe /
Nippon Design Center, Inc.

TITLE Design no Polylogue
PUBLISHER Seibundo Shinkosha Publishing Co., Ltd.

デザインのポリローグ　日本デザインセンターの50年

日本デザインセンター（NDC）の最大の財産は人である。創立から50年の間に、NDCは数々の人材を輩出してきた。NDCの歩みは日本のデザイン界で活躍する人々の歩みでもある。日本のデザインとともに歴史を刻んできたNDCの仕事とその歩みを再確認すると同時に、今後の日本のデザインとNDCの未来を、この集団にいた／いる人々との対話・ポリローグによって見通していく。

デザインのポリローグ　日本デザインセンターの50年

Yoshiaki Irobe /
Nippon Design Center, Inc.

95

TITLE Go Hasegawa: Conversations with European
Architects PUBLISHER LIXIL Publishing

長谷川豪　カンバセーションズ
ヨーロッパ建築家と考える現在と歴史

あなたの想像観、歴史観を決められてください。

新しさの正当性とは、それに必要とされないという事実に基づいているのです。（アルチザロ・シザ）
私はどなにも信じたい、私の建物も信念ときません。（ライバラ・オルジアティ）
ルネサンスと現代の建築の道いは、現代のほうが快適だということだけです。（ハーバー・メルテ）
より早いことは、より悪きなること、経済的は建築の材料です。（アンネ・ラカトン＆ジャン・フィリップ・ヴァッサル）
大地、建物、人間、都市、そこに新旧のジレンマに隔らないシートガントも選ずれます。（ABde・ブラバー）
古典的であり続けること、それは様式ではなく〈教理です。（ヴァレリオ・ゴールス＆ディルド・ファン・ゴーヴェレン）

LIXIL Publishing

中房総国際芸術祭いちはらアート×ミックス2014
Naka-boso International Art Festival ICHIHARA ART×MIX 2014

ICHIHARA ART×MIX

晴れたら市原、行こう
課題解決型芸術祭
いちはらアート×ミックスの全貌

Yoshiaki Irobe /
Nippon Design Center, Inc.

96

TITLE Ichihara Art×Mix 2014
PUBLISHER Gendaikikakushitsu Publisher

美しいデザイン
7人の女性アートディレクター
その視点と考え
ペンライト編

平林奈緒美
長嶋りかこ
福岡南央子
帆足英里子
宮田裕美詠
程藜
高井薫

PUBLISHER Seibundo Shinkosha Publishing Co., Ltd.

TITLE Utsukushii Design

TITLE Nendo in the Box
PUBLISHER ADP Company, Art Design Publishing

nendo
in the box

TITLE 1st Beijing Photo Biennial
PUBLISHER China Photographic Publishing House

灵光与 AURA &
后灵光 POST AURA

Wenbin Han / WX-Design

影舞之眼
视域之外
VISIONS & BEYOND

2ND SHENZHEN INDEPENDENT ANIMATION BIENNALE

第二届深圳独立动画双年展

董冰峰 何金芳 主编
Edited by Dong Bingfeng & He Jinfang

第二届CAFAM双年展 THE 2ⁿᵈ CAFAM BIENNALE

无形的手：策展作为立场
THE INVISIBLE HAND: CURATING AS GESTURE

中国青年出版社

Wenbin Han / WX-Design

104

TITLE The Invisible Hand
PUBLISHER China Youth Publishing Group

方正字库

方正字库
FOUNDER

Wenbin Han / WX-Design

105

TITLE Fangzheng Fonts Manual

PUBLISHER Beijing Founder Electronics Co., LTD.

TITLE A Little Melancholy
PUBLISHER Unitas Publishing Co.

TITLE A Little Alone
PUBLISHER Unitas Publishing Co.

TITLE A Gold Digging Story

PUBLISHER Unitas Publishing Co.

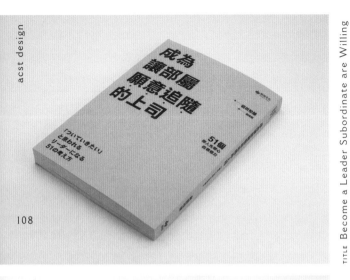

TITLE Become a Leader Subordinate are Willing to Follow PUBLISHER Delight Press

TITLE Affections for Food
PUBLISHER Delight Press

停下來，
讓靈魂跟上
就能呼喚
幸福。

徐小為——譯
丁稀在——著

活在當下，
什麼都不做
的權利

給總是
聽到「加油！」
的你——

我們都得了必須努力的病。
讀好大學、工作卓越、追求財富，
難道這一生都將如此美麗而脆弱的存在著？

唯有從「不前進就無法幸福」的焦躁感中脫身，
我們才能從原點重新自我審視、享受人生。

丁稀在

TITLE The Right to do Nothing
PUBLISHER Delight Press

dp 悅知文化

Index